The Ultimate Guide For Starting an Amazon Kindle Publishing Business

Step By Step Instructions How To Publish A Book, Promote It And Make Sales

Liudas Butkus

http://easym6.com

Introduction

Since I was a kid I was interested in writing books.

I remember writing silly little stories, drawing illustrations for them and then forcing my parents to read them.

I was particularly inspired by Harry Potter when I was in second grade and that lead me to writing at least 20 to 30 pages of a book. Luckily, Amazon Kindle didn't exist back then and I didn't get it published. That would have been embarrassing lol.

Amazon has really done a great job at simplifying the process of publishing a book. You no longer need to search for a publisher to get your work out there, no fees to pay, nothing.

All you need is to write the book and go through the simple process of filling out the publishing form on KDP. Who knows maybe next week your book will be a world-wide sensation.

However, if you would like to make money publishing books I would recommend choosing a different strategy, which isn't luck based – start an Amazon Kindle publishing business.

By starting a publishing business you won't need to pray to the gods to enlighten you with a book idea that's even creepier than Game of Thrones, instead you will be publishing books that people are already looking to read, you will be looking for demand and filling it by writing a book.

Sounds good?

Then continue reading, because here's what you will learn:

- The strategy for coming up with book ideas that sell.
- How to write a book or outsource it cheaply.
- How to get your book published on Amazon and look like a million bucks.
- The methods for promoting your book and getting it in the hands of thirsty readers.
- Closely guarded secrets that give you an edge over your competitors.

Picking a Profitable Niche

I doubt I can say anything new about picking a niche, every single internet marketing expert has covered this and if you already have picked a niche, then please go ahead and skip this part, if not, then keep reading.

If you want to build a striving publishing business, you want to enter a big, broad niche with millions of hungry buyers. We aren't worried about competition, because it's better to have a small piece of a big pie than a big piece of a small pie.

Obviously, the best niche to enter is something you have some experience with. Think about your interests, your hobbies, your expertise. What do you love doing and what you would enjoy learning more and teaching others about.

You should write a short list of interests and then evaluate them one by one, if they are good niches to go for.

Some topics that I'm currently learning about and I'm interested in:

- o Juicing/healthy diet
- o Investing
- o Animation
- o Freelancing
- o Working Abroad

Once you have a list you want to do a quick evaluation.

For example purposes, I have picked investing.

A good place to start your research is the Amazon Bestsellers list http://www.amazon.com/best-sellers-books-Amazon/zgbs/books/

If there are books in your niche that are selling well, then it's definitely a worthwhile niche. We only want to figure out, if there are buyers in your niche.

Obviously investing is a huge topic and there are a lot of books about it, but generally you want to drill down a bit, because it's easier to get into a smaller market segment. Let's say we want to write about forex trading.

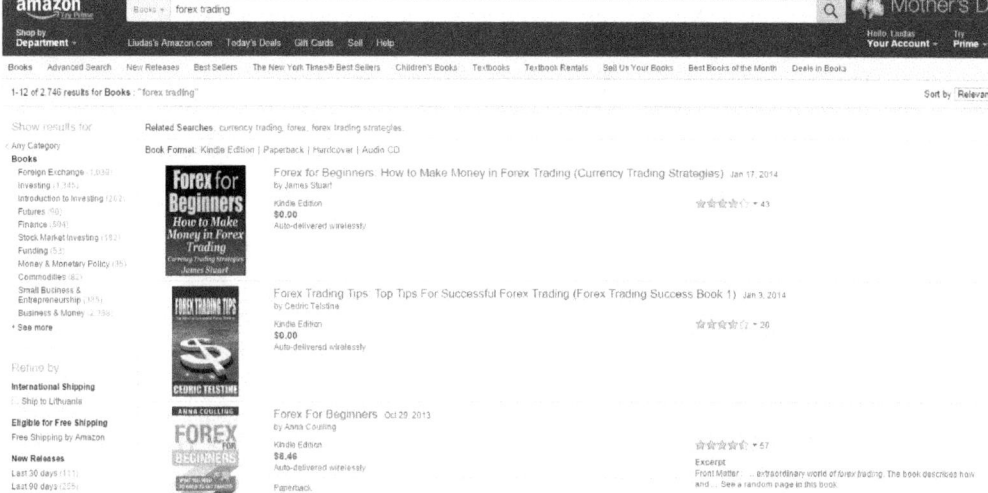

On the first page we can find a couple of free books, several high rated books and one bestseller that has a rank of #11,000, which means that it has to be making a lot of sales. Based on this I would be confident that there's a market for books about forex trading.

Don't Limit Yourself

When picking a niche don't limit yourself to internet marketing, health & wellness and self-improvement. Sure these are the niches that are huge and many people start in them and just niche down to a sub-niche, but there are plenty of other niches you could get into.

Less known niches have less competition and can have plenty of buyers, that could make it far easier for you to make money, but in the end it's up to you to make a choice. You don't want to enter a niche you hate.

Learn About Your Niche

If you picked a niche that you know little or nothing about, then you definitely need to spend time and educate yourself about it. The best and cheapest way is to find all the popular blogs in your niche and start reading them.

"niche + blog" search on Google will uncover plenty of blogs in your niche to get started. From the initial list of blogs, you will learn about other blogs, websites, books, movies, etc.

For example, type in "forex trading blog".

Forex traders - Plus500.com
www.plus500.com/**Forex-Trader** ▾
No Commissions. Signup Bonus! CFD **Trading**-Your capital is at risk
Plus500 has 2,677 followers on Google+

Plus500™ online forex trading - Plus500.lt
www.plus500.lt/ ▾
Prekiauti **Forex**, Akcijos, Indeksai CFD. Jūs rizikuojate savo kapitalu
Maži kursų skirtumai · Geri kursų skirtumai · Įrašytas į LAB · CFD tiekėjas
Plus500 has 2,677 followers on Google+
Indeksai CFD - Žaliavos CFD - Akcijos CFD - Pradėti prekybą

Forex - admiralmarkets.lt
www.admiral**markets.lt/Forex** ▾   (8-5) 210 4841
Padidink savo prekybos potencialą Gauk iki 50% depozito priedą!
Nemokami seminarai · Profesionali prekyba · Patikimas brokeris
Išbandykite dabar - Mokymai ir seminarai

<u>The Best Forex Blogs To Follow In 2014 - MahiFX</u> ⇐
https://mahifx.com/best-forex-blogs-2014/ ▾
A complete guide to the best **forex trading blogs** on the web. See if your favourite is on the list and get voting!

Forex Blog — Forex Trading Blog - EarnForex
www.**earnforex**.com/**blog**/ ▾
This Forex **blog** is used to share my **Forex trading** experience and any Forex related information that can help the currency traders.

Forex Blog Updates: FX Currency Trading News, Tips ...
www.babypips.com/**blogs** ▾ BabyPips.com ▾
Setting stop losses and profit targets with your **forex** EA usually entails a few more extra steps than just putting a value or variable in the parameters. Here's what ...

No Brainer Trades | Price Action & Systematic Forex Trading ...
www.nobrainer**trades**.com/ ▾
Price action trading strategy **blog** for discretionary and systematic **forex traders**.
Providing free education & instruction for beginner to advanced OTC and ...

The first result is a list of 50 blogs that you should follow, that's more than enough to get started.

Just by spending a good month learning about your niche you will know more than 99% of the people do.

Generating Ideas For A Book

Knowing your topic isn't enough you want to go deeper. You want to enter the conversation inside your customers minds.

To do that you need to go where they are discussing your topic, that would be forums and social media groups. You want to analyze the questions that people are asking, what problems do they have and obviously your book should be the solution.

Take note of all the ideas that come to mind. You need a ton of ideas because we won't be publishing just one book, if you want to make money you need to continuously publish high-quality books.

So, you will be going through this process of generating ideas over and over, but for now you only need a single good idea to go to the next step.

Some questions that people in forex trading ask:

- How to set-up my broker account?
- What is the best broker?
- Where can I get trading signals?
- How to read the charts?
- How to use indicators?

We can take some of these questions and transform them into books, but before we do that we want to do a final evaluation.

Evaluating Your Book Idea

Naturally when writing a book you think you need to come up with a completely unique idea, something that people haven't read, something that would shock them, but remember we aren't publishing novels here, you don't need to write the next Harry Potter.

What you do need is to provide the information that people are looking for and the main part for evaluating your idea is to research is there a critical mass looking for what you are offering.

Let's go to Google trends and search for the keywords that we discovered from the questions. We want to see, if there's a broader interest in that topic and also google trends will uncover other related terms that might help us.

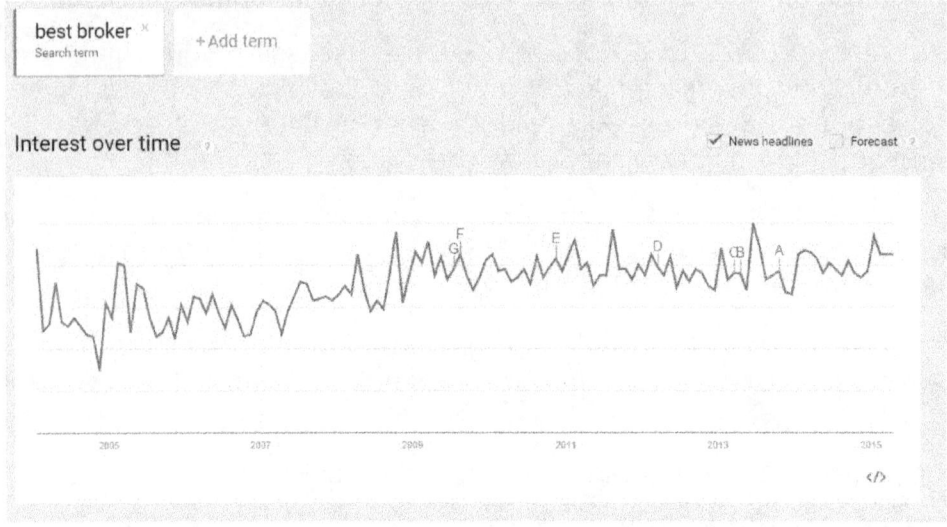

There's a pretty huge interest for the term best broker, but the term is a bit vague.

Topics	Top	Rising		Queries	Top	Rising
Investing online - Profession	25			best online broker	100	
Stockbroker - Occupation	25			online broker	100	
Mortgage broker - Bank	15			the best broker	95	
				stock broker	90	
				best stock broker	90	
				best forex broker	75	
				best forex	70	

If we scroll down we see "best forex broker" and that's a term that's very specific and here's its trend line:

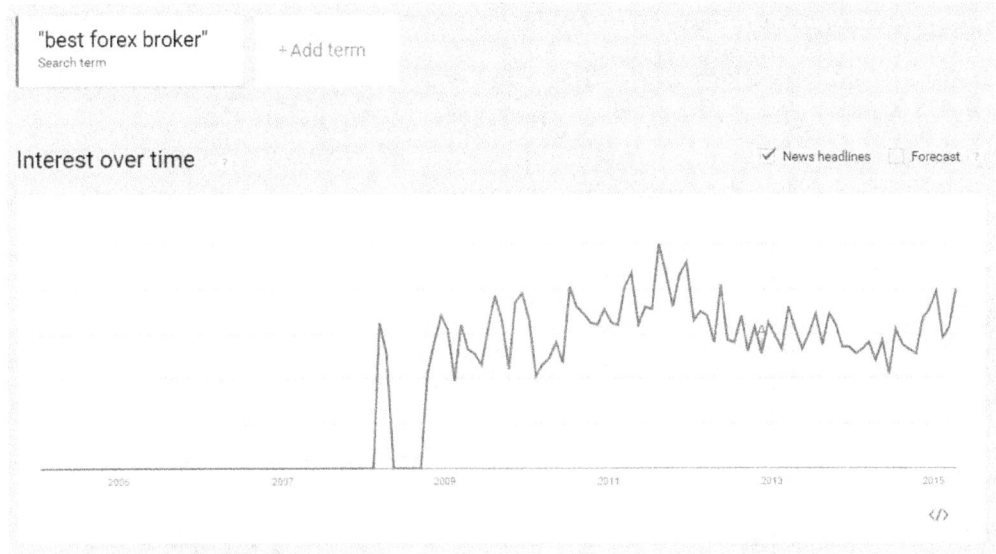

Interest over time

2006   2007   2009   2011   2013   2015

</>

It's clear there's still a lot of interest in it so, it would be a good topic to go for. However, it might not be broad enough to write a whole book about it so combining some other related topics would be a good idea.

Lastly, I would go to Amazon one more time to check, if there are books on exactly the same topic you're going to cover, if there are and they are selling well, then you have a green light for your idea. If there are books, but they aren't selling well, then analyze why, maybe they are just poorly written or there aren't enough buyers in which case you got a red light.

And if there aren't any books on your specific topic, then there are two possible reason why: no one has written about it yet, or no one is actually interested in that, though if there's a lot of interest on Google and on social media, then it's unlikely.

How To Write a Book?

We have done our research and made sure there are people willing to pay money for information on your topic. You now got two choices: Either write the book yourself or to outsource it.

Writing Yourself

If you're confident enough that you can write a book and you have the required knowledge, then by all means write it. However, if you picked a topic that is new to you, then just a month learning your topic might not be enough so, I would recommend spending at least a couple more months learning.

By writing yourself you save money and create a brand for yourself which helps you sell your books.

You probably expect that I'm now going to give you a secret formula for writing a book, but well there aren't any, you just need to find the time and do it. Still, here are some steps that will help you:

1. **Do Your Research:** Start off by reading everything you can find on your topic. Note some interesting stuff you learn, what are the common misconceptions about your topic, what are the main things that a person needs to know, etc. Again, how much research you need to do depends on how much you already know.
2. **Write The Outline:** When you have all those ideas flying in your head, you need to somehow catch them and put them in order. Writing an outline will help you do that. It's your plan for the whole book. When you have an outline writing becomes a breeze.
3. **Your First Draft:** You have the outline laid down, you now need to fill out all the chapters. Don't write and edit at the same time, it's a very common mistake that makes writing very slow and painful. Just write what comes to mind, don't overanalyze it.
4. **Editing:** The first step of editing is reading your whole book and fixing mistakes, the structure of sentences and paragraphs. All in all shaping your work into something readable, because if you followed the advice of not editing while you write, then you ended up with some really messy text. Second phase of editing is reading your book out loud and polishing the flow of your

book. If you are a perfectionist, I allow you to go through a third round of editing, but after that we are done, okay?

Outsourcing

There are plenty of places where you can go to outsource your book writing. Where I recommend you to go is either Elance.com or Freelancer.com.

There are plenty of writers on these sites and your job is to find the perfect one. You need to be very strategic when hiring to attract just the right people.

- **List out the skills you require the writer to have.** You want your writer to be knowledgeable about your topic and not just research everything after they got the job.
- **Write some requirements.** You want native English speakers who can write without mistakes, though you probably can get the job done cheaper, if you hire nonnative speakers. You might require applicants to have a specific star rating.
- **Mention how much you are willing to pay.** $15 or more for 1000 words is what you should expect paying.
- Let them know when you want the book written.
- **Ask for some extras.** You can also include a requirement that the writer needs to format the book for Kindle and CreateSpace, more on that later.

Also, before posting your listing check out other job offerings and analyze their structure. You might want to copy some elements to improve your listing.

Obviously the more you are willing to pay, the more applicants you will get. Having very specific requirements will make the job of screening through all the writers easier.

When screening your applicants you want to look at their ratings, you want to look at their previous jobs, how much they have made, etc. You only want to hire the best so, you won't waste your money on poor writing.

Once you got the book written, make sure it's high quality, if not send it back for revision.

Third Secret Method

Okay, okay, I said there's only two ways for writing a book, but I have actually come up with a third hybrid model. It involves just a little bit of writing from your part, a little bit of creativity and the majority of the content will be written by other people for free. Click here to find out more about this!
http://easym6.com/products/handsfreepublishing/html/

Formatting Your Book

For your book to look good on Kindle devices or when it's printed you want to have it properly formatted. If you outsourced the writing process, you can as well ask your outsourcer to have it formatted for you, just mention that in your job description.

But if you wrote your book yourself here's what you should keep in mind:

- You don't need to include a book cover image.
- The first page has to contain your Title, Subtitle and author name.
- Use page breaks to go to the next page.
- Second page should be interactive table of contents. When you click a chapter name it has to bring you to that chapter in the book. In Microsoft Word you can do it easily inserting table of contents. Also, **it's important to write interesting chapter names** because people often look at the TOC and decide whether to buy your book or not.
- Have an introduction to your book.
- Start a chapter by writing a heading, then write all your content in a single font (Calibri, Verdana, etc.). If you paste in text from other documents chances are they came with different formatting. You want to have consistent formatting through out the book. At the end of the chapter use a page break.
- Have an about the author section at the end of your book.
- Have a copyright notice at the end of your book.
- When using images in the book make sure to not resize them inside Word. It might cause errors. Use an image editor to resize them before inserting in the book.

Now, if you are having troubles with formatting the book, you can try out liber.io It's a tool that does all the necessary formatting for your document.

You just need to upload it and adjust the settings. It's free to use. (use screenshots and step by step instructions)
Sign up and you will land on a page like this. Click the huge plus sign to pick a method for uploading your document:

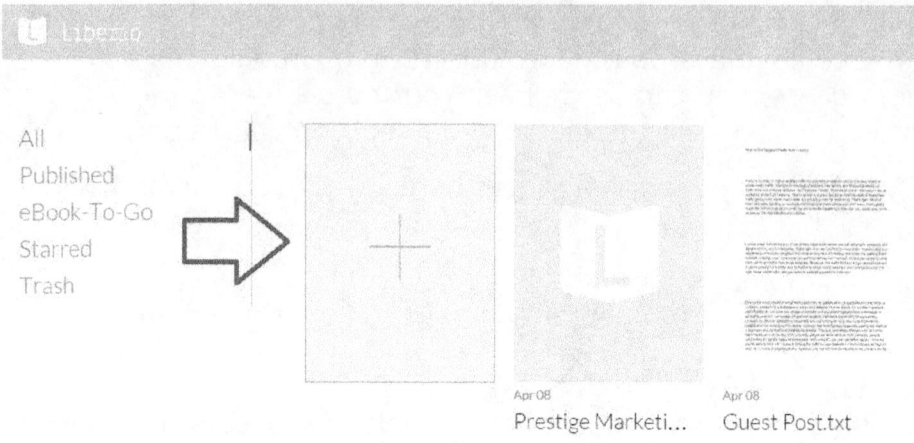

All
Published
eBook-To-Go
Starred
Trash

Apr 08
Prestige Marketi...

Apr 08
Guest Post.txt

On the next page, click more options to find all the necessary settings:

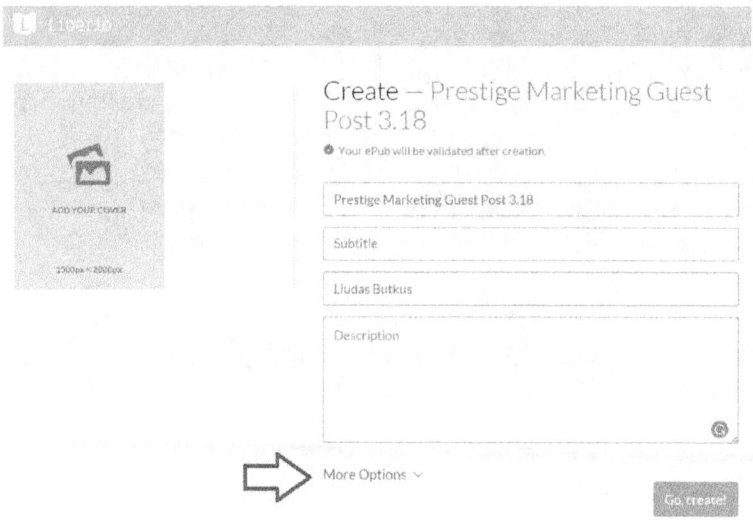

For the table of contents pick all the headings you want to include. Styling, pick the one you prefer. License and rights choose "All rights reserved" and all other fields can be left untouched.

Designing a Book Cover

Your book cover attracts people to your sales page. It's what helps you stand out in the crowded Amazon store. Now, it's not end all be all, but it's freakin important.

So, you shouldn't outsource this task to your kids. It's best to get a great design done, if you want to make serious sales of your book.

99designs.com

On 99 Designs you can start a competition for a book design. You get tons of designers competing for your work and you get to pick which one you like best. It can be a bit expensive, but you can be sure that you will get a design that you love.

If you have the money to invest, then this is the best way to go, but usually if you are publishing your first book you don't want to invest several hundred dollars into a cover, because you might not earn that back.

Fiverr.com

If you are on a budget and need the job done fast, then look for some talent on Fiverr. To get something better than just a stock template be ready to pay a bit more than $5.

Amazon Book Cover Creator

Empty pockets and no design skills? Check out the Amazon book cover creator. It's available when uploading your book. It's a straight forward editor that can help you get a cover done in minutes.

However, the covers turn out quite ugly and a lot of people use the same templates. So, a person who has been browsing the Amazon bookstore for a while won't take you seriously.

For now, I don't recommend using it, but maybe in the near future it will get updated and will be a splendid tool.

DIY (Design It Yourself)

I love to design my own book covers, can't say I'm the pro, but I do have some skills. If you have the guts to create the design yourself, then here are a few things that can help you.

Firstly, the cover should be 2820 pixels wide and 4500 pixels tall for the best looking result. The formats allowed are JPEG and TIFF. The book cover has to contain a Title, Subtitle and the Author's name.

For image editing, I recommend to choose something cooler than MS Paint. A simple tool with the core image editing features is pixlr.com. It's web based, so you won't need to download anything and it's free as well.
Go get your hands dirty with pixels!

Publishing The Book on Amazon Kindle

Open this site https://kdp.amazon.com/ , watch the short animation to get inspired and register for a KDP account, without one you can't publish.

Once you're done you will land on a page that looks something like this:

kindle direct publishing   **Bookshelf** | Reports   Community | KDP Select

---

(i)   Welcome to your new Bookshelf!

We're testing an improved Bookshelf and hope you enjoy the new look. As we test, you may see this Bookshelf or the earlier version.

New Title Checklist:

- **Book Content:** You will be asked to upload your manuscript in a recommended format. We recommend using Kindle content creation tools to create children's books, educational content, comics and manga.
- **Book Cover:** Use our online Cover Creator, or upload your cover in a supported format.
- **Description, Keywords and Categories:** Tell readers about your book and help them find it on Amazon.

See all Getting Started tips ›

Click add new title and you will get on the page for publishing your book.

Step 1	Step 2	Optional
Your book	**Rights & Pricing**	**KDP Select Benefits**
i Not Started...	i Not Started...	

Introducing KDP Select

Take advantage of KDP Select, an optional program that makes your book exclusive to Kindle and eligible for the following benefits:

- **Reach more readers** - With each 90-day enrollment period, your book will appear in Kindle Unlimited in the U.S., U.K., Italy, Spain, Germany, France, Brazil, Mexico and Canada and the Kindle Owners' Lending Library (KOLL) in the U.S, U.K., Germany, France, and Japan which can help readers discover your book.
- **Earn more money** - Every time your book is selected and read past 10% from Kindle Unlimited or borrowed from KOLL, you'll earn your share of the monthly KDP Select Global Fund. You can also earn a 70% royalty for sales to customers in Japan, Brazil, India and Mexico.
- **Maximize your sales potential** - Choose from two promotional tools including: Kindle Countdown Deals, time-bound promotional discounts for your book, available on Amazon.com and Amazon.co.uk, while earning royalties; or Free Book Promotion, where readers can get your book free for a limited time.

Learn more

☐ Enroll this book in KDP Select

By checking this box, you are enrolling in KDP Select for 90 days. Books enrolled in KDP Select must not be available in digital format on any other platform during their enrollment. If your book is found to be available elsewhere in digital format, it may not be eligible to remain in the program. See the KDP Select Terms and Conditions and KDP Select FAQs for more information.

Getting Started

Learn more about Kindle content creation tools for children's books, educational content, comics and manga.

1. Enter Your Book Details

Book name

New Title 1

Please enter the exact title only. Books submitted with extra words in this field will not be published. [Why?]

Subtitle (optional)

Please enter the exact subtitle only. Books submitted with extra words in this field will not be published. [Why?]

Firstly check the box that says "**Enroll this book in KDP Select**". By doing that you agree that your book will only be published on Amazon for the next 90 days and for that you will get the KDP marketing tools, which we will cover later on.

You don't want to mess with Amazon. I got one of my books taken off the KDP select program because it was available on other stores.

All the other stuff is pretty self-explanatory, but let's go through everything in order so, no stone gets unturned. We will also cover the important parts in more depth later on.

Book name – enter the book name.
Subtitle – it's optional, but you would be silly not to have one.

Edition number – if you are planning to publish several similar books and make them into a series, then you can give the series a name here.

Publisher – I leave this blank, but if you happen to have a publisher, you would enter it here.

Description – here you need to write a description about your book.

Book contributors – here you want to choose "author" and write in your name or a pen name. If it's a multi author book you can list out everyone as contributors.

Language – choose the language of the book.

ISBN – you can purchase an ISBN number and type it in, if you want. Amazon gives the instructions if you hover over the field. Normally you just publish without one.

Publishing rights – check "This is not a public domain work and I hold the necessary publishing rights."

Categories – choose two categories that best fit your book.

Age range – If your book is targeted for a specific age range you should set the age range. Normally, just leave it as is.

US. Grade range – If you are writing for specific grades, according to their reading level you can target that as well. Normally, just leave it as is.

Search keywords – type in 7 keywords that people would be likely to type in, if they were looking for your book.

Select your book release option – you can set it to publish right now, or on a set date.

Upload or Create a Book Cover – You can upload the book cover file or use the cover creator to create it.

Upload Your Book File – upload your book file :D.

Select a digital rights management (DRM) option – DRM means that people won't be able to copy your book and share it with others. I don't enable it, but you can choose to use it.

Continuing on to the second page...

List Building Strategies That Work

Step 1	Step 2	Optional
Your book	**Rights & Pricing**	**KDP Select Benefits**
✓ Published and available for purchase	/ In progress	

8. Verify Your Publishing Territories

Select the territories for which you hold rights: (What's this?)

- ● Worldwide rights - all territories
- ○ Individual territories - select territories

Select: All | None

- United States
- United Kingdom
- Guernsey
- Isle Of Man
- Jersey
- Canada

Regional territories: (0 of 245)

9. Set Your Pricing and Royalty

KDP Pricing Support (Beta)

See the relationship between price and past sales and author earnings for KDP books like yours.

[View Service]

KDP Pricing and Royalty

⚠ Effective January 1, 2015, list prices for EU marketplaces include VAT.
Learn more about VAT

Please select a royalty option for your book. (What's this?)

- ○ 35% Royalty
- ● 70% Royalty

FAQs

How do I identify my territorial rights?
If you hold worldwide rights, choose the worldwide rights option. If you do not hold worldwide rights, identify the specific territories for which you do have rights.

How much will I make when my book is sold?
You can choose between two royalty options: a 70% royalty option and a 35% royalty option. For example, for sales in the US, if your book's list price is between $2.99 and $9.99, you can choose the 70% option. The 35% option is available in the US for books with list prices between $.99 and $200.00. For complete information on royalty options, please see our Pricing Page and Terms and Conditions.

What is the delivery cost for?
Delivery costs vary based on the size of the book and apply if you select the 70% Royalty Option for your book. When you enter your list price in the Choose Your Royalty box, you will see the delivery cost associated with this book. If you select the 35% royalty option, delivery costs do not apply. For more information, see the Pricing Page.

Verify Your Publishing Territories – You can choose in which countries your book will be available for purchase. Worldwide is the way to go.

Set Your Pricing and Royalty – I go for only two types of pricing either $0.99 or $2.99. $0.99 can get you far more sales, but you will get only 35% royalty. When you pick $2.99 you get 70% royalty and that gets you $2 per sale. Feel free to experiment with higher prices as well.

Kindle Matchbook – this allows to offer your kindle version for people who bought your print version, if you have one.

Kindle Book Lending – it's what it sounds, your buyers will be available to lend your book to their friends for 14 days.

Once you've gone through all this, agree with the terms and click save and publish. It will take around 24 hours for your book to get approved and appear on Amazon.

Optimizing Your Book Listing

We already covered the bare minimum you need to know to publish your book, but anyone can figure out the bare minimum. You do want to be ahead of the crowd, right?

From here on I will cover advanced strategies that will give you an edge over your competition.

Writing a Powerful Description

Your description is somewhat a mini sales letter for your book. You shouldn't leave it at two sentences as most people do.

Amazon allows you to have up to 4000 characters so, you better make sure to use them. A simple template that works is a short **introduction** of the book, **bullet points** that cover unique things people will learn from the book, they have to make people curious about your book and **call to action** to go buy your book now.
Also, you can use simple HTML tags to format your description like <h1>, <h2>, <b>, <ul>, etc.

Categories

It's crucial to pick the right categories. It can be confusing because the names of the categories that you can choose are completely different from the ones that appear on Amazon.

It can be a pain in the ass looking for the two perfect categories, but take your time. If you get your book published and you see that the categories that you choose sound completely differently on Amazon, then feel free to choose different ones.

Some people browse for books using categories so, by doing this right you will have the chance to appear in front of them.

7 Pillars To More Sales

You can have up to 7 keywords for your book, it would be silly typing in only a few. By typing a keyword you're basically saying to Amazon that I want when people search for this term for my book to appear.

If it was just so simple, then you would type in the most popular keywords and you would enjoy the sales coming in, but of course other people are also competing for a spot on those keywords and if there are a lot of established books for a keyword then your chances of ranking for it are slim.

You need to look for high volume low competition keywords. Here's how you can find them:

Start out by typing in a keyword for your book on Amazon. You can immediately see auto suggestions:

If there's an auto suggestion for a keyword it means it has high search volume. That's one of the things we are looking for, but we also need to check if the competition isn't too high.

1-12 of 293 results for **Books** : "blogging for profit"

At the corner we can see how many books are competing for that keyword. Less than 10 000 books is a good number. Next, you need to go through several of the book listings and check their Amazon best selling rank.

Amazon Best Sellers Rank: #12,076 Paid in Kindle Store (See Top 100 Paid in Kindle Store)
#3 in Books > Computers & Technology > Internet & Social Media > **Blogging & Blogs**

From 1 to 100 000, the books are usually selling well and it's hard to compete with them. Also, take into account their reviews. If the whole page is filled with books that have rankings ranging **from 1 to 500 000** then it's usually a high competition keyword and you shouldn't use it.

If only a few books have rankings from 1 to 500 000 and others have rankings higher than 1 000 000, then it's a keyword where you have a chance to compete in and you should use it in your listing.

The truth is you might not find 7 perfect keywords, you might need to go for the high competition keywords as well.

After a few weeks, you want to go through your keywords and see how well you are ranking, if you aren't showing up on the first page, then the keywords isn't doing you any good so, you might consider replacing it.

Keyword Stuffing

A lot of marketers swear that keyword stuffing works on Amazon, but honestly I'm not a big believer of this because I haven't seen significant improvements in rankings after filling my description and titles with keywords.

Still, I encourage you to try it for yourself.

Bringing Your Book To Life

Publishing an ebook is a completely different feeling from publishing a physical book that you can take in your hands, squeeze it, open it and put it in a bookshelf.

You probably had a dream to publish a book, but publishing an ebook didn't really cut it for you, did it? Well, I'm going to show you how to publish a physical book pain-free using CreateSpace and how to make more money from your book sales by doing that.

Firstly, create an account at https://www.createspace.com/ it's an Amazon company so most of the things that we will need to do will be similar. You do need to provide tax information just like you did on KDP.
Once you have filled out all the boring information, you can advance to the fun stuff – publishing your book.

Start a new project and you will see a page like this:

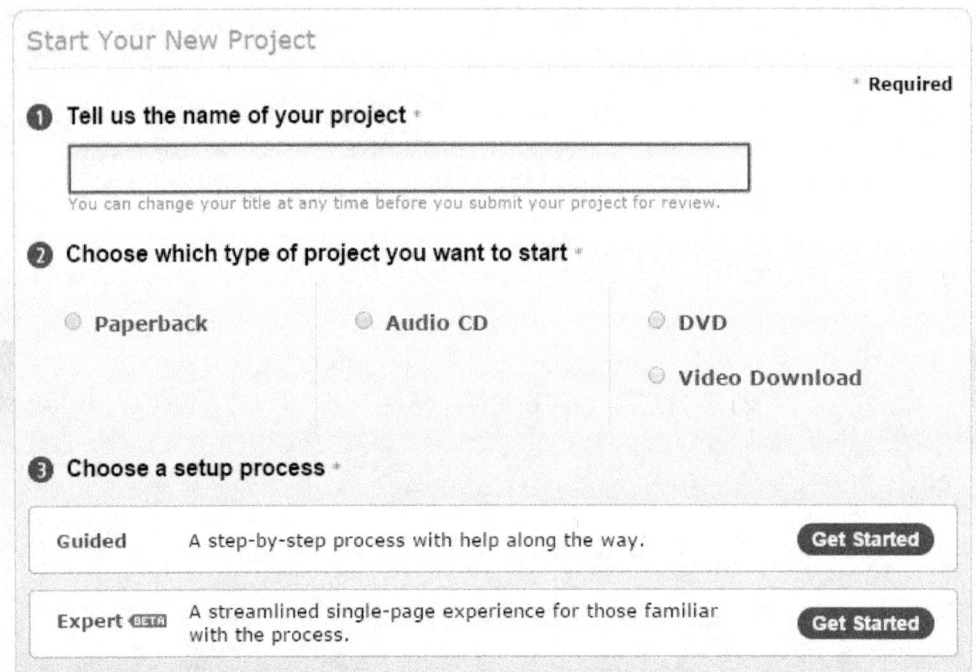

Tell us the name of your project – Paste in the title of your book.

Choose which type of project you want to start – As you can see CreateSpace can help you publish different products, something to keep in mind for the future, but for now you want to chose paperback.

Choose a setup process – Choose guided to go through the listing step by step.

Next you will land on something like this:

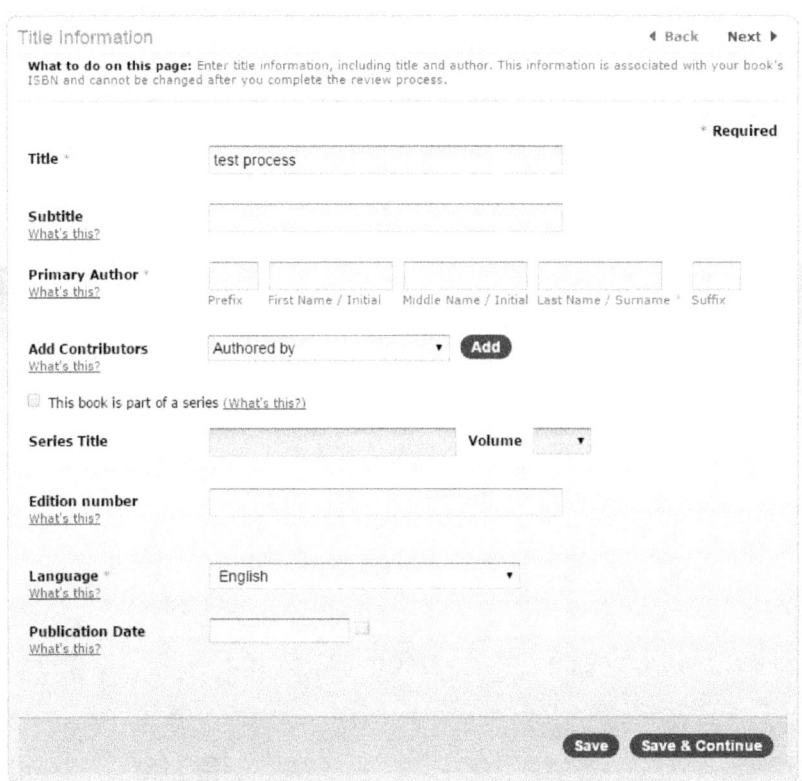

Again very basic stuff. Just use the same information you used for your Kindle book.

Next you will land on a page where you will need to get an ISBN number for your book. Don't worry Amazon will give you one for free.

Once you have your ISBN the next step is to set up your book content.

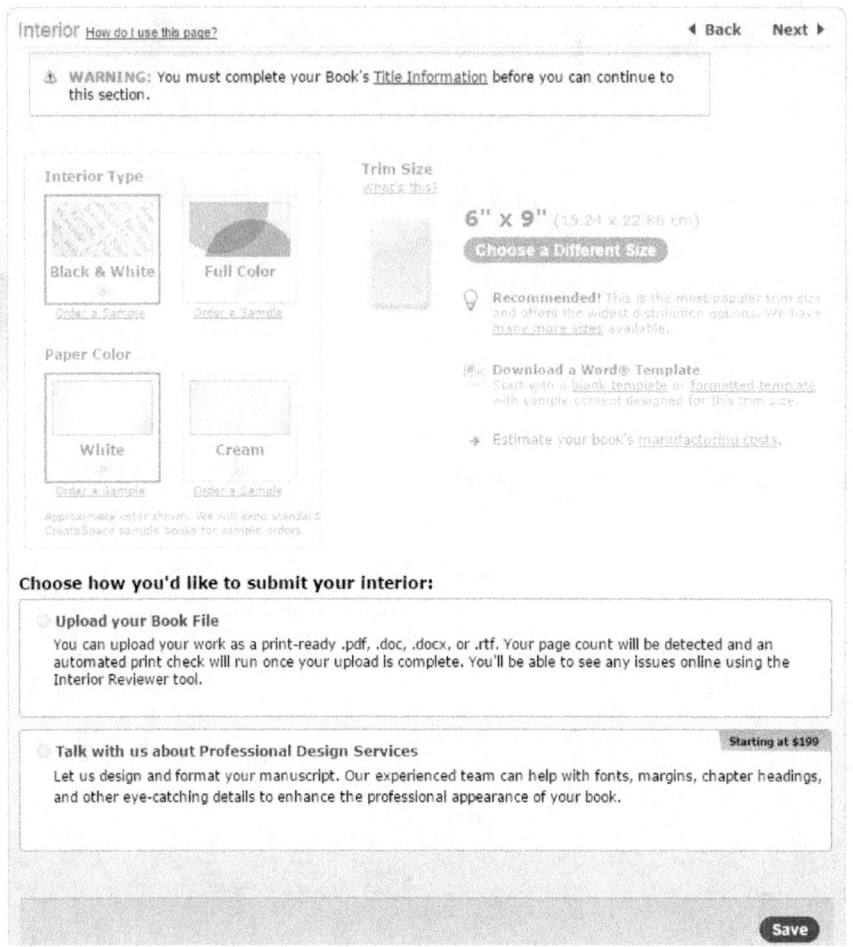

CreateSpace requires different formatting than a Kindle Book, but I did use the same file and used their auto-correction tool, "paste it into a template", to make it look good.

If you do find problems, you might need to play around with it.

The formatting of your book depends of the type of book you choose there are plenty to choose from, but I recommend the 6 x 9.

Also on the same page you can choose, if you want your book to be black and white or in color and the paper white or cream. Obviously the more fancy your book is the more it will cost to print.

Lastly, before we go to the next step, if you are writing very short books, then you won't be able to publish them. The minimum number of pages is 24.

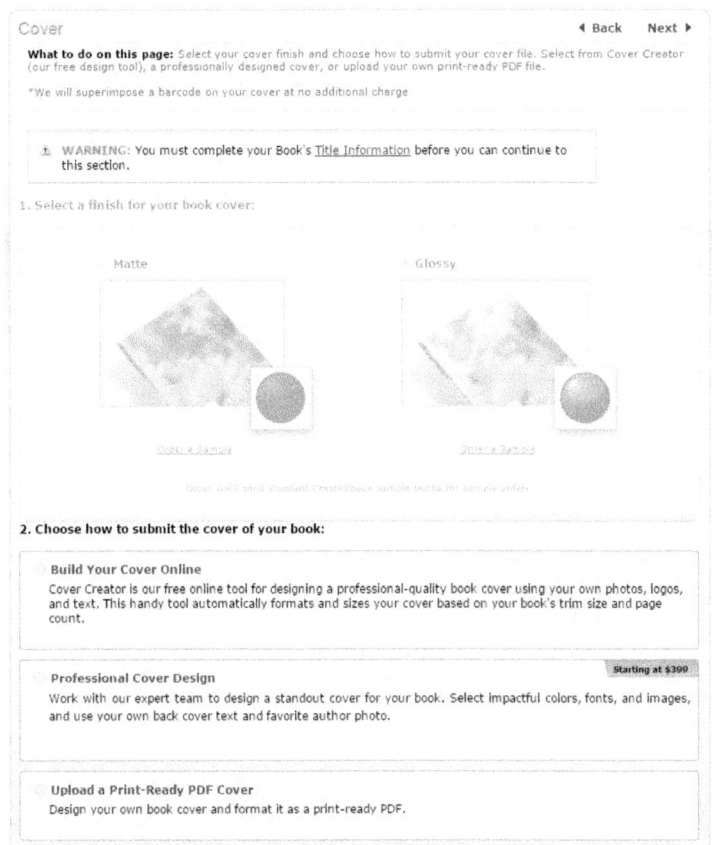

The cover on CreateSpace is going to be different, than on Kindle. You need the front, back and a spine, if your book is "fat" enough. An easy solution to this is contacting your designer and asking them to design another cover for you that works for CreateSpace.

It won't take long to design because they will be just adding to your original design and you will be up and running. There's also a free cover creator available on CreateSpace, but they look just as good as a birthday greetings card from a kindergartener.

If you would be designing the cover yourself, you can find templates right here:https://www.createspace.com/Help/Book/Artwork.do Lastly, pick the style for the cover glossy or matte.

Whew.

Now, submit the book for review and within 12-24 hours your book will be reviewed. If there are any errors you will be informed about them, if not you can then preview your book. you can view the digital version or you can buy a copy of your brand spanking new book. How cool is that?

For the preview you have two options: you can view the digital version or you can buy a copy of your brand spanking new book. How cool is that?

Once you reviewed your book and made sure it has swag, you are only a few clicks away from having your book published.

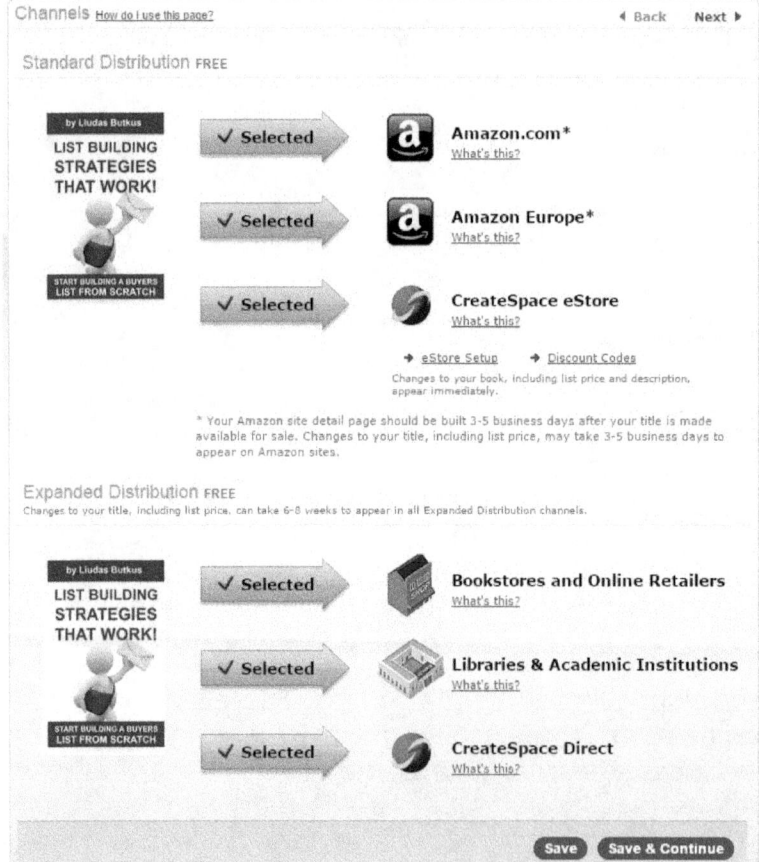

What you need to do now, is to choose the channels for distribution, if you have your book already published on Kindle,

Amazon will update your listing with a paperback in several days. Be patient here. I recommend choosing all the channels.

Pricing How do I use this page?
Set your list price and calculate your royalties for each sales channel and manufacturing location.
How are the royalties calculated?

◄ Back   Next ►

List Price			Channel	Royalty
$ 6.99 USD*	Calculate		Amazon.com	$2.04
Minimum list price for this title is $5.38 What's this?			CreateSpace eStore	$3.44
			Expanded Distribution	$0.64
☐ Yes, suggest a GBP price based on U.S. price What's this?				
£ 4.75 GBP**	Calculate		Amazon Europe For books printed in Great Britain	£1.77
Minimum list price for this title is £2.75				
☐ Yes, suggest a EUR price based on U.S. price What's this?				
€ 6.58 EUR**	Calculate		Amazon Europe For books printed in continental Europe	€2.89
Minimum list price for this title is €3.30				

Save   Save & Continue

* U.S. Price is required for all titles, even if U.S. channel is not enabled.
** Value Added Tax (VAT) is not included in the price. Appropriate VAT will be added to the price before the book is published. Learn more about VAT.

You also need to pick a listing price. I would go for $2 royalty for you. Remember that your buyers will also need to pay for shipping so, by keeping your price low you are making it more attractive.

Congratz, you have published a print book, I'm proud of you ☺

Generating Reviews

Imagine this scenario, a potential buyer lands on your book listing, he was impressed by your cover and that led him here in the first place, he read your description and it's just what he was looking for, he scrolls through the first pages of your book and he's optimistic about what's inside.

Lastly, he scrolls to the bottom and sees a single one star review bashing your book and he bounces.

Ouch, you just learned about the power of reviews. A single bad review can have your book sent to oblivion.

However, if you have 5 positive reviews and only a single negative review, then the story is a lot different.

The key to success is to get some positive reviews from the very beginning. LibraryThing.com is a great place for generating reviews. You won't need to bother your friends, you will be getting reviews from people who are interested in your book.
You will be doing a giveaway of your book in exchange for reviews. So, firstly register for account on Libraryhing and then follow this link: https://www.librarything.com/er/giveaway/list and then click post a giveaway.
To post a giveaway you will need to either be a LibraryThing Author, Have 50 Books in your librarything account or a paid library thing account. You can get approved for the LibraryThing author status in a day, if you have a book published on Amazon, which you will have by now, if you followed the steps.

Add book to Member Giveaways

Username	Liudas
Title	
Author name	
	Author's name in Last, First format.
Publisher	
Book URL	http://
	Can be publisher or author site.
Format	◉ paper book ○ eBook ○ audiobook
	If an ebook, be sure to read the rules about eBooks in the green box to the right.
ISBN	
Custom cover?	Upload my file Or grab one from the web
	Choose File No file chosen http://
Sale or release date	
	Must be in MM/DD/YYYY format.
Giveaway start date:	Choose duration ▾
	Must be in MM/DD/YYYY format. Giveaway will begin in 5 minutes if you choose today's date.
Number of copies available	
	Ebook giveaways are limited to 100 copies.
Countries you can send books to	Select (all countries | all EU countries)
	☐ USA ☐ UK ☐ Australia ☐ Germany
	☐ Canada ☐ Israel ☐ France ☐ Other

Posting a giveaway is very easy, you will use basically all the info you used for your listing. The only difference is that you are writing a description for you giveaway instead of your book.

Also, you will need to set how long you want to run a giveaway and how many copies you want to giveaway. Running it for a week and giving away a fairly limited amount of copies is the way to go.

After a week has passed you will get a list of all the winners. You will need to contact them personally and send them a copy of your book. Also, make sure to include a link to your kindle book page so, they can leave a review.

Generally people here are very nice and if they think critically of your book they won't publish a negative review or will give you tips to improve it.

Amazon's Top Reviewers

Another place to look for people to review your book is http://www.amazon.com/review/top-reviewers. It's a list of top reviewers on Amazon. These are people who enjoy getting free stuff for writing reviews.

Browsing through the whole list can be a bit challenging. The main criteria is that a person needs to have an email address listed. This means that he is open to contact.

Next, you want to make sure that the person has reviewed books before, most of the reviewers are interested only in physical goods to review so, they might not be interested in reviewing a book.

Lastly, you want to make sure the person is leaving only good reviews. If the person is only bashing all the stuff, then chances of getting a positive review are slim, but if he is leaving 4-5 star reviews, then if he doesn't like your book he might agree to not publish a review at all.

The top reviewers are very influential people and getting a review from them can give a huge boost to your book, but generally it's harder to get reviews from them.

Facebook Groups

Lastly, to get some quick reviews you can join "kindle review" groups on Facebook. It's far simpler and faster than starting a giveaway on LibraryThing or contacting top amazon reviewers.

The main con here is that these reviews can be a bit spammy because mainly people in these groups are authors themselves who are looking to promote their book. So, make sure you ask them to leave a honest review

Continuous Stream Of Reviews

The methods we already covered will help you get the initial reviews that help your sales, but you also want one last thing in place, which will help you generate more book reviews through the coming months and years.

And it's very simple, you want to ask for reviews inside your book. Have a short sentence at the end of your book "If you enjoyed this book please leave a review on Amazon". Chances are that if they made it till the end, then they have liked it and they will be glad to leave a review.

KDP Promotion Strategies

Hope you paid attention when we covered how to publish a book on Amazon and enrolled your book in the KDP Select Program. If not then you won't be able to use the promotion tools that Amazon gives you.

Let's quickly cover the promotion methods and when they are used.

Free Book Promotion

This is the main promotion method. It allows you to give away your book for free for 5 days, they don't need to be consecutive you can do 2 and 3 days or 5 times for 1 day, etc. Though I have seen best results by giving away my books from Monday to Friday.

It's best to use a free promotion for books that are new or aren't selling very well. It's not a good idea to use it for books that are selling well, because it can hurt your sellers rank.

If you followed the previous steps correctly, you have a great looking book listing and several reviews, then you can expect to get several hundred free downloads.

You might be wondering what's the point of giving away those books for free?

- More people learn about you and your other books
- People who read your book for free can still leave a review
- Based on how well your book performs on the promotion, your paid ranking will increase after
- You will build an audience, more on that later

You can do a free book promotion every 90 days and boost your book, but if your book is selling well, then you want to use...

Kindle Countdown Deals

If you have a book that's already selling a few or more copies a day and you notice that the sales start to slow down, you can do a Kindle Countdown Deal and offer your book at a discounted price for up to 7 days.

When using a countdown deal you don't get a lot of extra exposure, so again your book needs to be selling well to make it worthwhile using. The countdown deal only adds scarcity to your listing, which increases conversions.

Also, if you are selling your book for $2.99 and you do a countdown deal for $0.99 you will still get 70% royalties.

All in all, KCD are used by established authors.

Free Book Promotion on Steroids

People love free stuff and you can take advantage of that. There are a lot of reader communities that are looking for free books.

When your book is on a free kindle promotion you can submit your book to these communities and get a lot more free downloads.

Submitting your book to all these sites can take a lot of time so, you might want to only use the ones that provide the best results or outsource the submission process.

Go to: http://authormarketingclub.com/members/submit-your-book/ and register an account. When you scroll down to the bottom you will see a list of sites where you can promote your book. I have gotten the best results from AuthorMarketingClub, but feel free to submit to all of them.

Also, there are plenty of Facebook groups that allow to promote your free book. Just type in "free kindle books" and join as many as you like. Don't expect a lot from them because most of the groups consist of authors that are looking to promote their books. To make this process easy I recommend looking for a Facebook group auto poster.

Paid Promotion Strategies

A lot of the websites that allow you to submit your free books also allow you to promote your paid books to their audiences if you pay money. Now, it's hard to tell what kind of results you can get from a specific promotion because all the communities have different interests and some books can get great results while others will get nothing.

So, it requires some experimentation to see what sites get you results. Here's a list of sites where you can promote your book for several dollars.

Book Bub
Ereader News Today
Buck Books
Many Books
Kindle Nation Daily
The Kindle Book Review
Get Free Ebooks
Author Marketing Club
Obooko
Book Daily
Bargain eBook Hunter
Book Goodies
Awesome Gang
The Independent Author Network
Kindle Book Promos
Book Tweeting Service
GoodKindles
Daily Free eBooks
The Women's Nest
StoryFinds
Bibliotastic
Book Deal Hunter
Kufads

Remember just a few sales made from the promotion can increase the books sales rank and that can lead to even more sales so, when counting the ROI have that in mind.

As with all paid promotions start small and don't invest more than you are willing to lose.

Distributing Your Book On SmashWords

Amazon isn't the only ebook store out there. Sure, it's the biggest one and can bring the most sales, but distrubuting your ebook to other stores like Barnes & Noble, Apple store and others can also bring in additional sales.

Normally, you would do this when your book is already selling well and you are no longer interested in KDP promotion services, because if you publish your book on other stores you can no longer participate in KDP select. Make sure that you aren't in KDP select before you decide to distribute your books elsewhere.

To make the process of distributing your books as simple as possible I recommend usingSmashWords. You will need to set up your book with them once and then it will distribute your book to all the stores automatically.
It can take a few weeks for your book to appear in other stores.

Building an Email List

Would you like to be certain that every single book that you publish will perform better than the last one? Would be great, right? The more you publish the better results you get and well it's definitely possible.

How?

You need to build an email list. Now, what's a list? It's your audience that you can contact whenever you want. The bigger your list is the more influence you have. Imagine you publish a book and you send an email to 10 000 people. That would definitely bring some heat to your launch.

So, how do you get started?

Firstly, you need an autoresponder. I recommend using AWeber or GetResponse, but a lot of authors choose MailChimp because it's free until you reach 1 000 subscribers.

Next, you will need a squeeze page. A squeeze page is a page where people enter their email address to join your list. Here you have tons of options, but a free one that I recommend is http://kblm.co/ it quickly creates professional squeeze pages. For a squeeze page to work you need to give people a reason to subscribe. No one is going to submit their email just because they can, you need to give them a free gift in exchange for their email.

You can give one of your books for free if they subscribe or you can write a short report. Video training works as well. Just remember that you want to create a gift, which would be appealing to your audience.

If your books are in multiple niches, then you need multiple squeeze pages and build different lists.

Once you have a squeeze page you need to integrate it in your book to start getting subscribers. I recommend mentioning your bonus in the first ten pages and several times through out the book, if you think it adds to what you're talking about.

Make sure to type in the URL and not just hyperlink a word, because if someone buys your print book they won't be able to see the link.

Every single book that you publish will help you grow your email list and as your audience grows it will get easier and easier to promote your books.

Rinse And Repeat

We covered a lot right here. You now know how to publish a book and promote it to get the best results. The next step is to start writing your second book.

You won't get rich by just publishing one book, or two or three. Sure one lucky fellow might, but I don't believe in luck, it's far better to create your own luck and you can do that by constantly publishing new books.

You'll start seeing your royalty checks getting bigger and bigger with every new book that you publish.

Interlinking Your Books

When you have more than one book published you want to start interlinking them together. For easier navigation it's best to set up an author page with all your book titles and link to it within your books.

Go to https://authorcentral.amazon.com/ and sign-up for an account. It will set up a simple website for you that will have all your books listed.

There are many more benefits to setting up an author central. For example, on your book listings people will be able to see your author central and that gives a lot more credibility for your books.

Making Your Book Permanently Free

When you have several books published chances are that one of them won't be making any sales for you. You published a dud and you could potentially spend several hours tweaking and testing stuff to get it working, but there's no guarantee that you will make it happen.

A sure fire way to utilize books that aren't selling, is to set them free. Free like a bird. We already covered what good can a free book do to you, but with this strategy we aren't going to make the book free for 5 days, it's going to be forever.

To do that you need to make sure your book is no longer in KDP Select. Uncheck the mark from reenlisting your book and continue to the next step only when there's a week or two left before your current enlisting expires.

You need to make sure you aren't in the KDP Select because we are going to be publishing the book on other bookstores and that would be a violation of the TOS and several of these violations can get you banned.

So, how are you going to make your book free? Well, Amazon strives to have the lowest prices out there and for example, if you find an item on some other store cheaper than on Amazon, you can report the product to Amazon and it will match the price. This works with books as well.

SmashWords Again

Let's revisit the chapter about SmashWords, we will be using their platform to distribute our book to other stores and SmashWords allows to sell our book for $0. It can take several weeks until SmashWords will get your book published on iStore or Barnes & Noble, but be patient.

We need our book to get published on a reputable store for Amazon to notice. Sorry, SmashWords your store ain't good enough.

(2 – 3 weeks later)

You got your book published on at least one major ebook seller out there, it's time to let Amazon know about it so that it would price match the book.

I recommend singing up for KBoards (All things kindle forum) and finding a thread where people are reporting each others books to make them permanently free. You will need several people to report your book to make it free. Again, just as getting published, it can take even longer for Amazon to price match it.

(1-2 months later)
Your book is perma free and it's constantly bringing in some free downloads that may result in email subscribers and sales of your other books.

Finish or is it?

Congratulations on making through the whole book, you now know more than 99% of publishers on Amazon and that's a huge advantage to you.

However don't think that you don't need to be learning any more, the publishing business is evolving quickly and getting more competitive by the day so, you need to keep your knowledge fresh to stay on top.

Just by publishing new books you will learn a lot by what works and what doesn't and you will continue to get better.

All I can say right now is good luck and may the gods of productivity be with you.

Sincerely,

Liudas Butkus

http://easym6.com

P.S. To read more books from me check out:
http://www.amazon.com/Liudas-Butkus/e/B00NMSA2TQ/